THE MAKING OF A SLAVE

WILLIE LYNCH

For information regarding special discounts for bulk purchases,
please contact BN Publishing at
info@bnpublishing.net

www.bnpublishing.net

CONTENTS

This speech was delivered by Willie Lynch on the bank of the James River in the colony of Virginia in 1712. Lynch was a British slave owner in the West Indies. He was invited to the colony of Virginia in 1712 to teach his methods to slave owners there. The term "lynching" is derived from his last name.

Greetings

"Gentlemen, I greet you here on the bank of the James River in the year of our Lord one thousand seven hundred and twelve. First, I shall thank you, the gentlemen of the Colony of Virginia, for bringing me here. I am here to help you solve some of your problems with slaves. Your invitation reached me on my modest plantation in the West Indies, where I have experimented with some of the newest and still the oldest methods for control of slaves. Ancient Rome would envy us if my program is implemented. As our boat sailed south on the James River, named for our illustrious King, whose version of the Bible we cherish, I saw enough to know that your problem is not unique. While Rome used cords of wood as crosses for standing human bodies along its highways in great numbers, you are here using the tree and the rope on occasions. I caught the whiff of a dead slave hanging from a tree, a couple miles back. You are not only losing valuable stock by hangings, you are having uprisings. Slaves are running away. Your crops are sometimes left in the fields, too long for maximum profit. You suffer occasional fires. Your animals are killed. Gentlemen, you know what your problems are; I do not need to elaborate. I am not here to enumerate your problem; I am here to introduce you to a method of solving them. In my bag here, I HAVE A FULL PROOF METHOD FOR CONTROLLING YOUR BLACK SLAVES. I guarantee every one of you that if installed correctly IT WILL CONTROL THE SLAVES FOR AT LEAST 300 HUNDREDS YEARS. My method is simple. Any member of your family or your overseer can use it. I HAVE OUTLINED A NUMBER OF DIFFERENCES AMONG THE SLAVES; AND I TAKE THESE DIFFERENCES AND MAKE THEM BIGGER. I USE FEAR, DISTRUST

AND ENVY FOR CONTROL PURPOSES. These methods have worked on my modest plantation in the West Indies and it will work throughout the South. Take this simple little list of differences and think about them. On top of my list is "AGE" but it's there only because it starts with an "A." The second is "COLOR" or shade, there is INTELLIGENCE, SIZE, SEX, SIZES of plantations, STATUS on plantations, ATTITUDE of owners, whether the slaves live in the valley, on a hill, East, West, North, South, have fine hair, course hair, or is tall or short. Now that you have a list of differences, I shall give you an outline of action. But before that, I shall assure you that DISTRUST IS STRONGER THAN TRUST AND ENVY STRONGER THAN ADULATION, RESPECT OR ADMIRATION. The Black slaves, after receiving this indoctrination shall carry on and will become self refueling and self generating for HUNDREDS of years, maybe THOUSANDS. Don't forget, you must pitch the OLD black Male vs. the YOUNG black Male, and the YOUNG black Male against the OLD black male. You must use the DARK skin slaves vs. the LIGHT skin slaves, and the LIGHT skin slaves vs. the DARK skin slaves. You must use the FEMALE vs. the MALE and the MALE vs. the FEMALE. You must also have your white servants and over-seers distrust all Blacks. But it is NECESSARY THAT YOUR SLAVES TRUST AND DEPEND ON US. THEY MUST LOVE, RESPECT AND TRUST ONLY US. Gentlemen, these kits are your keys to control. Use them. Have your wives and children use them. Never miss an opportunity. IF USED INTENSELY FOR ONE YEAR, THE SLAVES THEMSELVES WILL REMAIN PERPETUALLY DISTRUSTFUL. Thank you gentlemen."

Let's Make A Slave

By The Black Arcade Liberation Library

It was the interest and business of slave holders to study human nature, and the slave nature in particular, with a view to practical results. I and many of them attained astonishing proficiency in this direction. They had to deal not with earth, wood and stone, but with men and by every regard they had for their own safety and prosperity they needed to know the material on which they were to work. Conscious of the injustice and wrong they were every hour perpetuating and knowing what they themselves would do. Were they the victims of such wrongs? They were constantly looking for the first signs of the dreaded retribution. They watched, therefore with skilled and practiced eyes, and learned to read with great accuracy, the state of mind and heart of the slave, through his sable face.

Unusual sobriety, apparent abstractions, sullenness and indifference indeed, any mood out of the common was afforded ground for suspicion and inquiry.

Frederick Douglas

LET'S MAKE A SLAVE is a study of the scientific process of man breaking and slave making. It describes the rationale and results of the Anglo Saxons' ideas and methods of insuring the master/slave relationship.

The Original and Development of a Social Being Called "The Negro."

Let us make a slave. What do we need? First of all we need a black nigger man, a pregnant nigger woman and her baby nigger boy. Second, we will use the same basic principle that we use in breaking a horse, combined with some more sustaining factors. What we do with horses is that we break them from one form of life to another. That is; we reduce them from their natural state in nature. Whereas nature provides them with the natural capacity to take care of their offspring, we break that natural string of independence from them and thereby create a dependency status, so that we may be able to get from them useful production for our business and pleasure.

Cardinal Principles for Making a Negro

For fear that our future generations may not understand the principles of breaking both of the beasts together, the nigger and the horse. We understand that short range planning economics results in periodic economic chaos; so that to avoid turmoil in the economy, it requires us to have breath and depth in long range comprehensive planning, articulating both skill sharp perceptions.

We lay down the following principles for long range comprehensive economic planning.

1. Both horse and niggers is no good to the economy in the wild or natural state.

2. Both must be BROKEN and TIED together for orderly production.

3. For orderly future, special and particular attention must be paid to the FEMALE and the YOUNGEST offspring.

4. Both must be CROSSBRED to produce a variety and division of labor.

5. Both must be taught to respond to a peculiar new LANGUAGE.

6. Psychological and physical instruction of CONTAINMENT

must be created for both

We hold the six cardinal principles as truth to be self evident, based upon the following the discourse concerning the economics of breaking and tying the horse and the nigger together, all inclusive of the six principles laid down about*.

Accordingly, both a wild horse and a wild or nature nigger are dangerous, even if captured, for they will have the tendency to seek their customary freedom, and in doing so, might kill you in your sleep. You cannot rest. They sleep while you are awake, and are awake while you are asleep. They are DANGEROUS near the family house and it requires too much labor to watch them away from the house. Above all, you cannot get them to work in this

* Neither principle alone will suffice for good economics. All principles must be employed for orderly good of the nation.

natural state. Hence both the horse and the nigger must be broken; that is breaking them from one form of mental life to another. KEEP THE BODY TAKE THE MIND! In other words break the will to resist. Now the breaking process is the same for both the horse and the nigger, only slightly varying in degrees. But as we said before, there is an art in long range economic planning. YOU MUST KEEP YOUR EYE AND THOUGHTS ON THE FEMALE and the OFFSPRING of the horse and the nigger. A brief discourse in offspring development will shed light on the key to sound economic principles. Pay little attention to the generation of original breaking, but CONCENTRATE ON FUTURE GENERATION. Therefore, if you break the FEMALE mother, she will BREAK the offspring in its early years of development and when the offspring is old enough to work, she will deliver it up to you, for her normal female protective tendencies will have been lost in the original breaking process. For example take the case of the wild stud horse, a female horse and an already infant horse and compare the breaking process with two captured nigger males in their natural state, a pregnant nigger woman with her infant offspring. Take the stud horse, break him for limited containment. Completely break the female horse until she becomes very gentle, where as you or anybody can ride her in her comfort. Breed the mare and the stud until you have the desired offspring. Then you can turn the stud to freedom until you need him again. Train the female horse where by she will eat out of your hand, and she will in turn train the infant horse to eat out of your hand also. When it comes to breaking the uncivilized nigger, use the same process, but vary the degree and step up the pressure, so as to do a complete reversal of the mind. Take the meanest and most restless nigger, strip him of his clothes in front of the remaining male niggers, the female, and the nigger infant, tar and feather him, tie each leg to a different horse faced in opposite directions, set him a fire and beat both horses to pull him apart in front of the remaining nigger. The next step is to take a bull whip and beat the remaining nigger male to the point of death, in front of the female and the infant. Don't kill him, but PUT THE FEAR OF GOD IN HIM, for he can be useful for future breeding.

The Breaking Process of The African Woman

Take the female and run a series of tests on her to see if she will submit to your desires willingly. Test her in every way, because she is the most important factor for good economics. If she shows any sign of resistance in submitting completely to your will, do not hesitate to use the bull whip on her to extract that last bit of bitch out of her. Take care not to kill her, for in doing so, you spoil good economics. When in complete submission, she will train her off springs in the early years to submit to labor when they become of age. Understanding is the best thing. Therefore, we shall go deeper into this area of the subject matter concerning what we have produced here in this breaking process of the female nigger. We have reversed the relationship in her natural uncivilized state, she would have a strong dependency on the uncivilized nigger male, and she would have a limited protective tendency toward her independent male offspring and would raise male off springs to be dependent like her. Nature had provided for this type of balance. We reversed nature by burning and pulling a civilized nigger apart and bull whipping the other to the point of death, all in her presence. By her being left alone, unprotected, with the MALE IMAGE DESTROYED, the ordeal caused her to move from her psychological dependent state to a frozen independent state. In this frozen psychological state of independence, she will raise her MALE and female offspring in reversed roles. For FEAR of the young males life she will psychologically train him to be MENTALLY WEAK and DEPENDENT, but PHYSICALLY STRONG. Because she has become psychologically independent, she will train her FEMALE off springs to be psychologically independent. What have you got? You've got the nigger WOMAN OUT FRONT AND THE nigger MAN BEHIND AND SCARED. This is a perfect situation of sound sleep and economic. Before the breaking process, we had to be alertly on guard at all times. Now we can sleep soundly, for out of frozen fear his woman stands guard for us. He cannot get past her early slave molding process. He is a good tool, now ready to be tied to the horse at a tender age. By the time a nigger boy reaches the age of sixteen, he is soundly broken in and ready for a long life of sound and efficient work and the reproduction of a unit of good labor force. Continually through the breaking of uncivilized savage nigger, by throwing the nigger female savage into a frozen psychological state of independence, by killing of the protective male image, and by creating a submissive dependent mind of the nigger male slave, we have created an orbiting cycle that turns on its own axis forever, unless a phenomenon occurs and re shifts the position of the male and female slaves. We show what we mean by example. Take the case of the two economic slave units and examine them closely.

The Negro Marriage Unit

We breed two nigger males with two nigger females. Then we take the nigger male away from them and keep them moving and working. Say one nigger female bears a nigger female and the other bears a nigger male. Both nigger females being without influence of the nigger male image, frozen with an independent psychology, will raise their offspring into reverse positions. The one with the female offspring will teach her to be like herself, independent and negotiable (we negotiate with her, through her, by her, negotiates her at will). The one with the nigger male offspring, she being frozen subconscious fear for his life, will raise him to be mentally dependent and weak, but physically strong, in other words, body over mind. Now in a few years when these two offspring's become fertile for early reproduction we will mate and breed them and continue the cycle. That is good, sound, and long range comprehensive planning.

WARNING: POSSIBLE INTERLOPING NEGATIVES

Earlier we talked about the non economic good of the horse and the nigger in their wild or natural state; we talked out the principle of breaking and tying them together for orderly production. Furthermore, we talked about paying particular attention to the female savage and her offspring for orderly future planning, then more recently we stated that, by reversing the positions of the male and female savages, we created an orbiting cycle that turns on its own axis forever unless a phenomenon occurred and resift and positions of the male and female savages. Our experts warned us about the possibility of this phenomenon occurring, for they say that the mind has a strong drive to correct and re-correct itself over a period of time. If I can touch some substantial original historical base, they advised us that the best way to deal with the phenomenon is to shave off the brute's mental history and create a multiplicity of phenomena of illusions, so that each illusion will twirl in its own orbit, something similar to floating balls in a vacuum. This creation of multiplicity of phenomena of illusions entails the principle of crossbreeding the nigger and the horse as we stated above, the purpose of which is to create a diversified division of labor thereby creating different levels of labor and different values of illusion at each connecting level of labor. The results of which is the severance of the points of original beginnings for each sphere illusion. Since we feel that the subject matter may get more complicated as we proceed in laying down our economic plan concerning the purpose, reason and effect of crossbreeding horses and nigger, we shall lay down the following definition terms for future generations:

1. Orbiting cycle means a thing turning in a given path.
2. Axis means upon which or around which a body turns.
3. Phenomenon means something beyond ordinary conception and inspires awe and wonder.
4. Multiplicity means a great number.
5. Sheer means a globe.
6. Cross-breeding a horse means taking a horse and breeding it with an ass and you get a dumb backward ass long headed mule that is neither reproductive nor productive by itself.
7. Crossbreeding niggers mean taking so many drops of good white blood

> and putting them into as many nigger women as possible, varying the drops by the various tones that you want, and then letting them breed with each other until another circle of color appears as you desire. What this means is this; put the niggers and the horse in a breeding pot, mix some assess and some good white blood and what do you get?

You got a multiplicity of colors of ass backward, unusual niggers, running, tied to a backward ass long headed mules, the one productive of itself, the other sterile. (The one constant, the other dying, we keep the nigger constant for we may replace the mules for another tool, both mule and nigger tied to each other, neither knowing where the other came from and neither productive for itself, nor without each other.)

The Negro Marriage Unit

Controlled Language

Crossbreeding completed, for further severance from their original beginning, WE MUST COMPLETELY ANNIHILATE THE MOTHER TONGUE of both the new nigger and the new mule and institute a new language that involves the new life's work of both. You know language is a peculiar institution. It leads to the heart of a people. The more a foreigner knows about the language of another country the more he is able to move through all levels of that society. Therefore, if the foreigner is an enemy of the country, to the extent that he knows the body of the language, to that extent is the country vulnerable to attack or invasion of a foreign culture. For example, if you take a slave, if you teach him all about your language, he will know all your secrets, and he is then no more a slave, for you can't fool him any longer, and BEING A FOOL IS ONE OF THE BASIC INGREDIENTS OF AN INCIDENTS

TO THE MAINTENANCE OF THE SLAVERY SYSTEM. For example, if you told a slave that he must perform in getting out "our crops" and he knows the language well, he would know that "our crops" didn't mean "our crops" and the slavery system would break down, for he would relate on the basis of what "our crops" really meant. So you have to be careful in setting up the new language for the slaves would soon be in your house, talking to you as "man to man" and that is death to our economic system. In addition, the definitions of words or terms are only a minute part of the process. Values are created and transported by communication through the body of the language. A total society has many interconnected value system. All the values in the society have bridges of language to connect them for orderly working in the society. But for these language bridges, these many value systems would sharply clash and cause internal strife or civil war, the degree of the conflict being determined by the magnitude of the issues or relative opposing strength in whatever form. For example, if you put a slave in a hog pen and train him to live there and incorporate in him to value it as a way of life completely, the biggest problem you would have out of him is that he would worry you about provisions to keep the hog pen clean, or the same hog pen and make a slip and incorporate something in his language where by he comes to value a house more than he does his hog pen, you got a problem. He will soon be in your house.

Printed in the USA
CPSIA information can be obtained
at www.ICGtesting.com
LVHW021955120923
757953LV00002B/22

9 781638 23087

The
Seven-Day Mental Diet

Dr. Emmet Fox

Dr. Emmet Fox
July 30, 1886- August 13, 1951

Dr. Emmet Fox was a new thought teacher, author, healer and minister, encouraging millions with his views of health, inner peace and success.

ISBN 978-1-60386-842-6

DIGITALIZED BY
WATCHMAKER PUBLISHING

It makes no difference how deeply seated may be the trouble, how hopeless the outlook how muddled the tangle, how great the mistake. A sufficient realization of love will dissolve it all.

The 7 Day Mental Diet

The subject of diet is one of the foremost topics of the present day in public interest. Newspapers and magazines teem with articles on the subject. The counters of the bookshops are filled with volumes unfolding the mysteries of proteins, starches, vitamins, and so forth.

The whole world is food-conscious. Experts on the subject are saying that physically you become the thing that you eat — that your whole body is really composed of the food that you have eaten in the past. What you eat today, they say, will be in your bloodstream after the lapse of so many hours, and it is your blood-stream that builds all the tissues composing your body — and there you are.

Of course, no sensible person has any quarrel with all this. It is perfectly true, as far as it goes, and the only surprising thing is that it has taken the world so long to find it out; but in this article I am going to deal with the subject of dieting at a level that is infinitely more profound and far-reaching in its effects.

I refer of course to "mental" dieting.

The most important of all factors in your life is the mental diet on which you live.

It is the food which you furnish to your mind that determines the whole character of your life. It is the thoughts you allow yourself to think, the subjects that you allow your mind to dwell upon, which make you and your surroundings what they are.

As thy days, so shall thy strength be. Everything in your life today — the state of your body, whether healthy or sick, the state of your fortune, whether prosperous or impoverished', the state of your home, whether happy or the reverse, the present condition of every phase of your life in fact — is entirely conditioned by the thoughts and feelings which you have entertained in the past, by the habitual tone of your past thinking. And the condition of your life tomorrow, and next week, and next year, will be entirely conditioned by the thoughts and feelings which you choose to entertain from now onwards.

In other words, you choose your life, that is to say, you choose all the conditions of your life, when you choose the thoughts upon which you allow your mind to dwell. Thought is the real causative force in life, and there is no other. You cannot have one kind of mind and another kind of environment. This means that you cannot change your environment while leaving your mind unchanged, nor — and this is the supreme key to life and the reason for this article — can you change your mind without your environment changing too. This then is the real key to life: *if you change your mind your conditions must change too.* Your body must change, your daily work or other activities must change; your home must change; the color- tone of your whole life must change, for whether you be habitually happy and cheerful, or low-spirited and fearful, depends entirely on the quality of the mental food upon which you diet yourself. Please be very clear about this. If you change your mind your conditions must change too.

We are transformed by the renewing of our minds.

So now you will see that your mental diet is really the most important thing in your whole life.

This may be called the Great Cosmic Law, and its truth is seen to be perfectly obvious when once it is clearly stated in this way.

In fact, I do not know of any thoughtful person who denies its essential truth. The practical difficulty in applying it, however, arises from the fact that our thoughts are so close to us that it is difficult, without a little practice, to stand back as it were and look at them objectively. Yet that is just what you must learn to do.

You must train yourself to choose the subject of your thinking at any given time, and also to choose the emotional tone, or what we call the mood that colors it. Yes, you can choose your moods. Indeed, if you could not you would have no real control over your life at all.

Moods habitually entertained produce the characteristic disposition of the person concerned, and it is his disposition that finally makes or mars a person's happiness.

You cannot be healthy; you cannot be happy; you cannot be prosperous; if you have a bad disposition. If you are sulky, or surly, or cynical, or depressed, or superior, or frightened half out of your wits, your life cannot possibly be worth living. Unless you are determined to cultivate a good disposition, you may as well give up all hope of getting anything worthwhile out of life, and it is kinder to tell you very plainly that this is the case.

If you are not determined to start in now and carefully select all day the kind of thoughts that you are going to think, you may as well give up all hope of shaping your life into the kind of thing that you want it to be, because this is the only way.

In short, if you want to make your life happy and worthwhile, which is what God wishes you to make it, you must begin immediately' to train yourself in the habit of thought selection and thought control.

This will be exceedingly difficult for the first few days, but if you persevere you will find that it will become rapidly easier, and it is actually the most interesting experiment that you could possibly make. In fact, this thought control is the most thrillingly interesting hobby that anyone could take up. You will be amazed at the interesting things that you will learn about yourself, and you will get results almost from the beginning.

Now many people knowing this truth make sporadic efforts from time to time to control their thoughts, but the thought stream being so close, as I have pointed out, and the impacts from outside so constant and varied, they do not make very much progress. That is not the way to work.

Your only chance is definitely to form a new habit of thought which will carry you through when you are preoccupied or off your guard as well as when you are consciously attending to the business. This new thought habit must be definitely acquired, and the foundation of it can be laid within a few days, and the way to do it is this:

Make up your mind to devote one week solely to the task of building a new habit of thought, and during that week let everything in life be unimportant as compared with that.

If you will do so, then that week will be the most significant week in your whole life. It will literally be the turning' point for you. If you will do so, it is safe to say that your whole life will change for the better. In fact, nothing can possibly remain the same. This does not simply mean that you will be able to face your present difficulties in a better spirit; it means that the difficulties will go. This is the scientific way to Alter Your Life, and being in accordance with the Great Law it cannot fail. Now do you realize that by working in this way you do not have to change conditions.

What happens is that you apply the Law, and then the conditions change spontaneously. You cannot change conditions directly — you have often tried to do so and failed — but go on the *Seven Day Mental Diet* and conditions must change for you.

This then is your prescription. For seven days you must not allow yourself to dwell for a single moment on any kind of negative thought. You must watch yourself for a whole week as a cat watches a mouse, and you must not under any pretense allow your mind to dwell on any thought that is not positive, constructive, optimistic, kind. This discipline will be so strenuous that you could not maintain it consciously for much more than a week, but I do not ask you to do so. A week will be enough, because by that time the habit of positive thinking will begin to be established. Some extraordinary changes for the better will have come into your life, encouraging you enormously, and then the future will take care of itself. The new way of life will be so attractive and so much easier than the old way that you will find your mentality aligning itself almost automatically.

But the seven days are going to be strenuous'. I would not have you enter upon this without counting the cost. Mere physical fasting would be child's play in comparison, even if you have a very good appetite. The most exhausting form of army gymnastics, combined with thirty-mile route marches, would be mild in comparison with this undertaking.

But it is only for one week in your life, and it will definitely alter everything for the better. For the rest of your life here, for all eternity in fact, things will be utterly different and inconceivably better than if you had not carried through this undertaking.

Do not start it lightly. Think about it for a day or two before you begin. Then start in, and the grace of God goes with you. You may start it any day in the week, and at any time in the day, first thing in the morning, or after breakfast, or after lunch, it does not matter, but once you do start you must go right through for the seven days. That is essential. The whole idea is to have seven days of unbroken mental discipline in order to get the mind definitely bent in a new direction once and for all.

If you make a false start, or even if you go on well for two or three days and then for any reason "fall off" the diet, the thing to do is to drop the scheme altogether for several days, and then to start again afresh. There must be no jumping on and off, as it were.

You remember that Rip Van Winkle in the play would take a solemn vow of teetotalism, and then promptly accept a drink from the first neighbor who offered him one, saying calmly: *"I won't count this one."*

Well, on the *Seven Day Mental Diet* this sort of thing simply will not do. You must positively count every lapse, and whether you do or not, Nature will. Where there is a lapse you must go off the diet altogether and then start again.

Now, in order, if possible, to forestall difficulties, I will consider them in a little detail.

First of all, what do I mean by negative thinking? Well, a negative thought is any thought of failure, disappointment, or trouble; any thought of criticism, or spite, or jealousy, or condemnation of others, or self-condemnation; any thought of sickness or accident; or, in short, any kind of limitation or pessimistic thinking.

Any thought that is not positive and constructive in character, whether it concerns you yourself or anyone else, is a negative thought. Do not bother too much about the question of classification, however; in practice you will never have any trouble in knowing whether a given thought is positive or negative. Even if your brain tries to deceive you, your heart will whisper the truth.

Second, you must be quite clear that what this scheme calls for is that you shall not entertain, or dwell upon negative things.

Note this carefully. It is not the thoughts that come to you that matter, but only such of them as you choose to entertain and dwell upon.

It does not matter what thoughts may come to you provided you do not entertain them. It is the entertaining or dwelling upon them that matters.

Of course, many negative thoughts 'will come to you all day long. Some of them will just drift into your mind of their own accord seemingly, and these come to you out of the race mind. Other negative thoughts will be given to you by other people, either in conversation or by their conduct, or you will hear disagreeable news perhaps by letter or telephone, or you will see crimes and disasters announced in the newspaper headings.

These things, however, do not matter as long as you do not entertain them. In fact, it is these very things that provide the discipline that is going to transform you during this epoch-making week.

The thing to do is, directly when the negative thought presents itself — turn it out. Turn away from the newspaper; turn out the thought of the unkind letter, or stupid remark, or what not.

When the negative thought floats into your mind, immediately turn it out and think of something else. Best of all, think of God as explained in The Golden Key.

A perfect analogy is furnished by the case of a man who is sitting by an open fire when a red-hot cinder flies out and falls on his sleeve. If he knocks that cinder off at once, w without a moment's delay to think about it, no harm is done. But if he allows it to rest on him for a single moment, under any pretense, the mischief is done, and it will be a troublesome task to repair that sleeve. So it is with a negative thought.

Now what of those negative thoughts and conditions which it is impossible to avoid at the point where you are today? What of the ordinary troubles that you will have to meet in the office or at home?

The answer is, that such things (negative experiences or conditions) will not affect your diet provided that you do not accept them, by fearing them, by believing them, by being indignant or sad about them, or by giving them any power at all.

Any negative condition that duty compels you to handle will not affect your diet. Go to the office, or meet the cares at home, without allowing them to affect you. (None of these things move me), and all will be well.

Suppose that you are lunching with a friend who talks negatively — do not try to shut him up or otherwise snub him. Let him talk, but do not accept what he says, and your diet will not be affected. Suppose that on coming home you are greeted with a lot of negative conversation — do not preach a sermon, but simply do not accept it.

It is your mental consent, remember, that constitutes your diet. Suppose you witness an accident or an act of injustice let us say — instead of reacting with pity or indignation, refuse to accept the appearance at its face value; do anything that you can to right matters, give it the right thought, and let it go at that. You will still be on the diet.

Of course, it will be very helpful if you can take steps to avoid meeting during this week anyone who seems particularly likely to arouse the devil in you. People who get on your nerves, or rub you up the wrong way, or bore you, are better avoided while you are on the diet; but if it is not possible to avoid them, then you must take a little extra discipline — that is all.

Suppose that you have a particularly trying ordeal before you next week. Well, if you have enough spiritual understanding you will know how to meet that in the spiritual' way; but, for our present purpose, I think I would wait and start the diet as soon as the ordeal is over. As I said before, do not take up the diet lightly, but think it over well first.

In closing, I want to tell you that people often find that the starting of this diet seems to stir up all sorts of difficulties.

It seems as though everything begins to go wrong at once. This may be disconcerting, but it is really a good sign. It means that things are moving; and is not that the very object we have in view? Suppose your whole world seems to rock on its foundations. Hold on steadily, let it rock, and when the rocking is over, the picture will have reassembled itself into something much nearer to your heart's desire.

The above point is vitally important and rather subtle. Do you not see that the very dwelling upon these difficulties is in itself a negative thought which has probably thrown you off the diet? The remedy is not, of course, to deny that your world is rocking in appearance, but to refuse to take the appearance for the reality. Judge not according to appearances but judge righteous judgment.

A closing word of caution: *Do not tell anyone else that you are on the diet, or that you intend to go on it.* Keep this tremendous project strictly to yourself. Remember that your soul should be the Secret Place of the Most High. When you have come through the seven days successfully, and secured your demonstration, allow a reasonable' time to elapse to establish the new mentality, and then tell the story to anyone else who you think is likely to be helped by it. And, finally, remember that nothing said or done by anyone else can possibly throw you off the diet. Only your own reaction to the other person's conduct can do that.

Printed in the USA
CPSIA information can be obtained
at www.ICGtesting.com
LVHW021955120923
757953LV00002B/23

9 781603 8684